The Music Coach

A Beginners Guide to Helping You Break into the Music Industry

Norris Spivey Jr

Norris@GreenwaveEntertainment.com
www.GreenwaveEntertainment.com

Copyright, Legal Notice and Disclaimer:

This publication is protected under the US Copyright Act of 1976 and all other applicable international, federal, state and local laws, and all rights are reserved, including resale rights: you are not allowed to give or sell this Guide to anyone else. If you received this publication from anyone other than Greenwave Entertainment Network, you've received a pirated copy. Please contact us via e-mail at info@GreenwaveEntertainment.com and notify us of the situation.

Please note that much of this publication is based on personal experience and anecdotal evidence. Although the author and publisher have made every reasonable attempt to achieve complete accuracy of the content in this Guide, they assume no responsibility for errors or omissions. Also, you should use this information as you see fit, and at your own risk. Your particular situation may not be exactly

www.GreenwaveEntertainment.com

suited to the examples illustrated here; in fact, it's likely that they won't be the same, and you should adjust your use of the information and recommendations accordingly.

Any trademarks, service marks, product names or named features are assumed to be the property of their respective owners, and are used only for reference. There is no implied endorsement if we use one of these terms.

Finally, use your head. Nothing in this Guide is intended to replace common sense, legal, or other professional advice, and is meant to inform and entertain the reader. So have fun with the "The Music Coach", and get noticed!\

© 2014 by Greenwave Entertainment Network, All Rights Reserved worldwide under The Music Coach may not be copied or distributed without prior written permission.

Copyright © 2014 Norris Spivey Greenwave Entertainment Network

www.GreenwaveEntertainment.com

All Rights Reserved Worldwide

About Greenwave

Norris Spivey was raised in a family with an abundance of musicians and artists, so naturally, his involvement with music was inevitable. Since an early age, music was a major part of his life, either by playing an instrument, producing tracks, or as part of a concert promotion team. With years of industry knowledge, Spivey is able to provide artists a winning edge.

"In every industry there are tips which are shared with certain people. Well, I will be giving you tips of the music industry and coaching you in advancing to your next level." ~ Norris Spivey, Jr.

Greenwave Entertainment Network, created by Spivey, assists new artists in multiple areas of music. Greenwave has collaborated with a team of industry professionals who collectively

www.GreenwaveEntertainment.com

possess many years of music experience. Greenwave's main purpose is to see you, the artist, succeed at reaching your goal of obtaining industry success.

Greenwave presents: The Music Coach. This is the primary resource that provides you with the necessary tools needed to advance your music career to the next level. By consulting with artists, mapping the position of your career, and providing strategic plans, The Music Coach, coaches you.

The Music Coach is remarkable by delivering personal and professional attention to the artist, every step of the way. There are many areas of focus when starting your music career. The Music Coach will not only focus on artist development, but also marketing techniques. There are several aspects to cover and The Music Coach will tackle them all.

www.GreenwaveEntertainment.com

"Just as the late, great Maxine Powell, who developed artists for Motown, The Music Coach's mission is very vital and guarantees to leave a lasting impression!" ~ Norris Spivey, Jr.

www.GreenwaveEntertainment.com

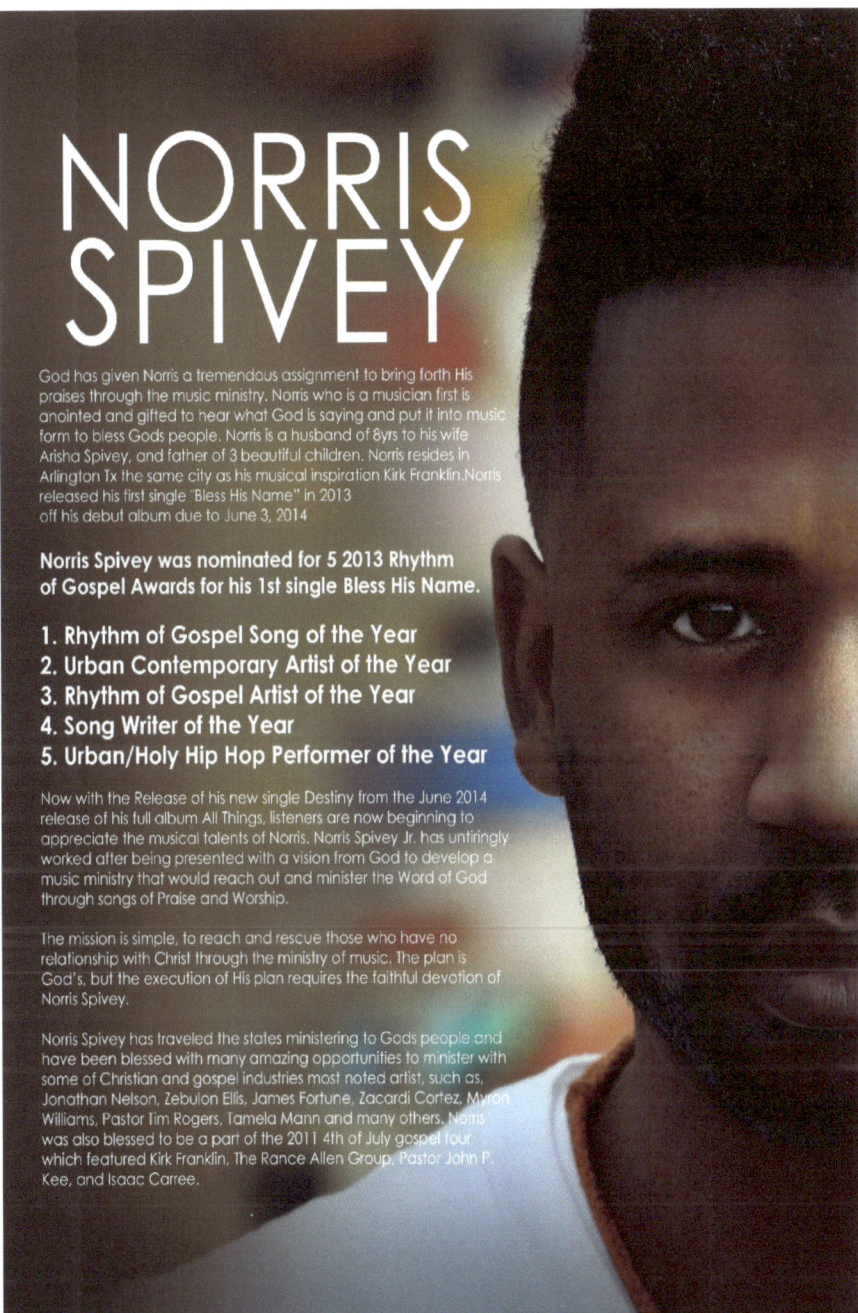

Table of Contents

Introduction……………………………………….10

Chapter 1 Creating Your Image………………..13

    Image Branding……………………………….13

    Identifying Your "IT" Factor…………………..16

    Utilizing Social Media……………………….19

Chapter 2 Appearances………………………..24

    Vocal Lessons………………………………24

    Artist Appearances…………………………29

        On Stage……………………………….29

        Off Stage……………………………….32

    Live Performances………………………….37

    Social Media…………………………………41

Chapter 3 Music Selection…………………….44

    Production……………………………………49

    Radio…………………………………………51

    Getting Your Fans Involved……………….56

www.GreenwaveEntertainment.com

Song Promotion..................................59

Chapter 4 Growth............................63

Why is the hard work worth it?..........68

What to expect next?........................73

Where would you be without this guidebook?..78

Chapter 5 Conclusion......................83

Can you answer these questions?....83

Your Next Steps...............................84

Glossary of Terms............................88

Artists Checklists.............................95

Album Checklist..............................95

Rehearsal Checklist.......................99

Performance Checklist..................100

Recording Checklist......................101

Budget Worksheet...........................103

www.GreenwaveEntertainment.com

Introduction

Thank you for taking the time to purchase this book. Be proud of yourself, you have just made a major first step in your music career!! After years of watching artists continue to release songs and albums resulting in no sales, low gigs, or maybe accomplishing only small local stardom, which quickly fades; I knew it was time to release The Music Coach to offer guidance and open their eyes to industry standards.

The first, most important, lesson you will learn with this book is the definition of the word "quality". Merriam-Webster® simply defines quality as: *"how good or bad something is"*. When I say quality, I'm not only speaking of a great mix and master, as it has many shares in the music industry. Quality can make or break you in an ultra-competitive environment. Being of "star quality" is at the top of the list of qualifications. Low quality in any market will

www.GreenwaveEntertainment.com

never be taken seriously, even if the product appears to have "star quality".

The second most important thing you, as a reader, will learn is to never give up. When you were created, you were given a gift, and if your gift is to sing or perform, then do it! Too often we have allowed others to define us or sway our decision on pursuing what has always been in our heart. When we are done, I want you to be full of confidence. I am going to coach you, so all I need from you is to be coachable. When you finish this book, you should be prepared to take the next step in your music career. You will be ready to take your music where it has never gone before. So singing in front of large crowds, hearing your music on the radio, and touring the country is your desire? You want to be a nationally recognized artist? Tell me, how do you intend to get there? What steps do you take, what producers will you use, what image do you want to portray? What is your first step?

www.GreenwaveEntertainment.com

All of these questions, and more, will be answered as you read further. My job, as a coach, is to ensure that when you are done with this book, you can answer these questions. Are you ready to begin your journey to a lasting and prosperous music career? Well, let's go......

www.GreenwaveEntertainment.com

Chapter 1 Creating Your Image

Image Branding

Before we begin to discuss image branding, we must first understand the definition of branding. **Branding** is what sets your feature apart from everyone else, your uniqueness. Branding describes you, as the product.

Branding is Chapter 1 for a good reason. Which normally comes first when purchasing an album: the picture on the cd cover or the sound? Exactly, the image, or the picture. The first part of image branding is knowing what to brand.

As an artist, you must first discover who you are, on and off the stage. Nothing is worse than a music artist "acting" while on stage, because of an image he/she is trying to fake. No one can beat you at being you, so capitalize and build on that premise. As an artist, you're just that, an artist. This means, if you are unsure on an appropriate image for you and your music, connect with an **image consultant**. Let the consultant get to know your personality, likes, and dislikes. They will need to hear your music, see your music videos, any live performances and how you interact with others in your day-to-day life. This is necessary to make certain your style is conveying the correct image.

Do not confuse your audience. I remember an artist cd cover, where he was wearing sun shades and a nice jacket, or blazer. He appeared laid-back, but once I heard his song, it was very "commercial" and "hyped". His music did not match his look, whatsoever. I thought it was going to be more of an R&B record. I was misled due to the image he portrayed on his cover. Be you, if you are a country singer; I should be able to look at your cd cover and know you're a country singer.

Image also means a "representation" of something. In this case, that something is you, the artist. Your image has to represent who you are and it should tell a story. An image should not be overly busy with excessive elements of color or text, this can be confusing. The goal is to be simple, but interesting.

Once you have determined the image which accurately defines you, contact a reputable photographer. Prior to hiring a photographer, preview their previous work or ask to see their **portfolio**. What you're looking for is clean professional photography. You need someone who actually has experience with music artists and not just a photographer with a camera. This process can either make or break a record.

Now that you have your photos, you will need to hire a professional **graphic designer**. The higher quality photos makes it much easier for your graphic designer to create your cd cover and your other marketing material, which we will cover in later chapters. Now that you have the perfect image which reflects you, as an artist, let's move on to the next step.

Identifying Your "IT" Factor

Each person was created with a special gift and personality. No two people are exactly alike. There is something unique in you, which sets you apart from the rest of the world. Some people may spend a lifetime trying to change their originality, because they may believe this isn't the most popular or acceptable, but it's who you are! In this section, you will identify your special trait, or your "IT" factor.

In this industry, **music executives**, like myself, are always looking for an artist who has great talent along with marketability. When going through thousands of demos, one thing we notice, are a lot of artists who believe they have discovered the perfect sound in which the industry desires. They spend their money and time creating a record mimicking another "A list" artist. This practice very rarely catches the attention of execs. The industry doesn't want to see a clone of an artist. Maybe a clone of success, but definitely not of artistry.

Fans will not respect a new artist that comes onto the music scene, looking and acting like their favorite artist.

~

"Remember, your fans can make or break you in the beginning of your career."

~

You may be thinking, but what about influences? This does not mean an artist is not affected by existing artists influence, those are needed and very helpful to grow music in general. We learn from previous generations and the stars who were produced during those times. But, there is a difference between mimicking, or copying, and being inspired or influenced by a legendary star. Mimicking is a false copy of the real thing. Being influenced inspires an artist and sparks a fire in your own gift and art, to create something magical. As an artist, you have to learn who you are and what your strong characteristics, or selling points. You may have to dig deep into your core and discover you're "It" factor.

How to begin searching for the staple, which will determine your "It" factor? When you start your search, go back, to when you first began. We tend to alter ourselves, our beliefs, our character, to become popular and noticed. I want you to go back to Day 1. Do you remember that thing you did, others didn't know how you did "it", or they were unable to do "it". "It" was something you could do without having to try hard. Some artists are strong, belting singers. Others may be very energetic on stage, while others may be great at high-pitched falsettos. Whatever you have discovered, make that your focus. Spend time with that and perfect "it". This is the true essence of you, as an artist.

Don't be afraid to ask those who have been with you from the beginning and those who will give you an honest answer. Ask them, *"what do you see as my "it" factor"*? Your "it" dynamic needs to be polished daily. You want to work "it" over and over and allow "it" to grow and expand. Whatever you do, make it great.

www.GreenwaveEntertainment.com

You will cherish and cultivate this until "it" blossoms into greatness. When you are ready for an audition, or into the studio to record a **demo**, you will know that the decision-makers want your "it" factor to be YOUR "it" factor and not just a cheap replica of another artist.

Utilizing Social Media

The music industry has dramatically changed over the past 14yrs. There are more artists releasing albums and songs today, than ever before. Growing up in the 80's, recording music was more of a strenuous process, than today. Recording at home was nearly impossible, therefore, the competition was kept at a minimum. When a new artist was signed to a record label, the most popular way he/she obtained fame and notoriety was either by word-of-mouth, headlining for another popular artist, or they simply heard the artist's premier song on the radio. Times have changed and the creation process of original music is much more "user friendly ". The music industry have evolved greatly with the digital programs made

www.GreenwaveEntertainment.com

available to anyone with a computer, which is practically every American.

The Apple Company®, released *Apple iTunes*®. This program allowed **digital downloading** of music from popular or brand new artists. Any artist who simply has a closet, in their home, and around $300 worth of *ProTools*® recording hardware and software, can place their recorded music online for digital uploading from fans. This enables anyone in the world immediate access to the artist's music. Because of this, the competition for new artist recognition is fierce!

There are more artists today releasing albums and singles, each Tuesday, than ever before. The internet enables an even playing field for artist. Those who are signed to a major label, may have executive dollars marketing and promoting their record. Today, recording music is very simple. With the available technology, music production and marketing, are cost-efficient. As an independent artist, or independent label, whose budget may be

www.GreenwaveEntertainment.com

substantially smaller than a major label, you too need to focus on marketing. There are a variety of marketing techniques, but the most cost effective method is utilizing major **social media** websites. Social networking sites, such as: *Facebook®, twitter®, Instagram®* and *YouTube®*, are among the most popular for promotion.

Let's start with when and what to post. Here's the scenario: You have decided to release a song this year, but you're not signed with a major label. Your optimal goal is to symbolize yourself as a signed artist with a major record label, backed by a major budget. This creates a competitive edge against major artists who are currently being acknowledged, recognized and followed.

6 – 8 months prior to album release date: Announce to everyone that you have started the recording process. Keep your fans updated. They may want to follow you "behind-the-scenes". Fans today have a desire to feel connected and close to the artists they support, but remember, to maintain a level of confidentiality. Don't show your audience EVERYTHING. Give them enough to keep them connected and interested, but not so much where they become comfortable or too familiar with you. Release a few photos of you, while in the studio recording. Also, upload any live performances. This will exemplify your greatness and relay to the audience that you are "official".

3 - 4months prior to album release date: You should have finished recording your music. It's now time to distribute **official marketing materials** to your social media audience. Select a date and create a release flier. As stated earlier; this is a job for an experienced graphic designer. If your release announcement is poorly done, your audience may believe your music is poorly done. Don't cut corners. You can even use the photos which were taken previously by the professional photographer. Your music release announcement, or flier, should contain your picture, an image of the theme your single or album will reflect, and all pertinent information on the release date. This needs to be *eye catching*, but not overly busy with a lot of unnecessary texts or graphics.

Upload short videos, where you are discussing the album, on your *Instagram*® and *Facebook*® profile. Tell your audience what to expect and post these videos consistently. Keep your music fresh in their mind.

1 month prior to album release date: Now is the time to share snippets, or small pieces, of the single. This should now be available for pre order. You can post a few bars of your new song to your *Facebook*®, *Instagram*® and *YouTube*® page. Continue to post this up until the release date. As a new artist, don't be afraid to ask your friends and followers for help. Ask them to repost your marketing material, if they like the song. Also, if your song is uploaded to *iTunes*®, ask followers and fans for a *5-star rating* and to post comments about your song. These ratings will influence purchases.

Chapter 2 Appearances

Vocal Lessons

The journey to becoming a great singer typically begins at a young age and leads up through adolescent years. Not everyone actually starts vocal training early in their lives, and if this describes you, be encouraged you still have time. No matter the level of your career, a great vocal coach can only help in your advancement. In this chapter, we discuss the importance of a great vocal coach or voice instructor.

A vocal coach is a person trained to help singers improve their performance and singing techniques. As a coach, they will show you ways in which to protect your voice and rid you of habits which can destroy your vocal cords. A great vocal coach can take your career to the next level, depending on your work ethic. When selecting a coach always ask for references, and contact them, to assist in the selection process.

A coach should evaluate where you currently need improvement, by listening and observing your vocal skills and performance techniques. Some coaches have earned professionally training, music degrees, or simply rely on their experience. As a student, you should always remain open to learning, but most importantly, have the willingness to take the lessons learned from your coach and practice when you're alone.

A lesson should be designed to provide you the tools needed to expand your vocal ability. Don't feel overwhelmed when starting your lessons, go in with an honest and realistic expectation. No two singers are alike. Once you begin lessons, you will learn that it takes time to change old habits which may have formed from years of singing, prior to any formal training.

A major problem which I have encountered, in this industry, is that most singers tend to lose their pitch. This is called a "pitchy" singer. Due to new digital pitch correction software, this is not as costly when recording in the studio. But live performances reveal your flaws all too well. Finding a coach who recognizes your flaws, identifies them, and offers effective solutions, is vital for your overall improvement. The only way to achieve growth, is with honesty. It may hurt at first, but you will thank them later.

Coaches have more responsibility than just teaching you about pitch and breathing. Some vocal coaches also assist in studio song production. This is something that I recommend for new and experienced artists. Also known as a vocal producer, their main purpose is to arrange background vocals and lead vocals in a way which compliments the song. They also assure of a current and exciting sound that motivates the lead vocalist to reach their highest level of excellence.

I always advise artists who are seeking to begin recording their demo or album, to find

www.GreenwaveEntertainment.com

a reputable vocal producer. The chosen producer should be willing to attend studio sessions with you and arrange the vocals. If you're a singer, sing! If he/she is a vocal producer, let them produce. This will encourage your focus on singing and creating music.

Additionally, ensure that you hire a vocal coach who has specialized training in speech and **diction**. Learn how to enunciate your words without compromising your originality. Your development should be customized to fit your voice and unique style. There's no better way to lose listeners than a new artist, with a new song, whose words are not understandable.

As a singer, myself, I am certain you have also asked this question, "Why does my voice continue to become hoarse and what do I do about it"? A vocal coach should have tips for this, but if it is something that occurs more often than not, then it may be your singing technique. We must keep in mind the tempos

www.GreenwaveEntertainment.com

and keys of songs that we sing. Get to know your voice and its limitations. This the most common aspect often overlooked.

Your vocal timbre and range changes throughout your life. Between your teenage years until your adult life, you will be able to sing notes which may challenge a much older singer. Constant strain can take a toll on your vocal cords. Always be sure you have a proper warm-up routine before utilizing your full voice. Vocal cords are made soft flesh, therefore, rest is imperative. They require proper care. This is your instrument.

Just as a keyboardist takes care of their piano; you must take special care of your voice. If your voice is showing signs of strain, take a break. Take a few days to rest your voice. Try to refrain from extensive singing and talking. Once you feel as though you are ready to begin singing again; limit the hours of singing for the next few days.

Whichever vocal coach you select, ensure they provide you with evaluations of your voice depth and guide you into full voice usage properly. As you continue looking for the right program, remember this, you want a coach that makes you feel comfortable and natural. You also should seek a coach who encourages the increase of your vocal range and adds a uniqueness to your sound.

If you are a singer who sings primarily loud and belting songs, then you may want to add more contrasting tones to give your listeners. This provides listeners an insight into your sense of emotions. While performing, many artists practice breathing and strength control, this should not restrict their vocal personality. In conclusion, you should have advanced knowledge of your vocal ability and a new sense of professionalism while caring for your instrument, your voice!

Artist Appearances

On Stage

As you progress in your career, you will begin to make appearances on and off stage. Both are equally important to your growth as an artist. Let's discuss on-stage appearances. You are totally responsible for the perception given to your fans and listeners. New artists, more importantly, have less room for error. When listeners see you for the first time, you must impress them. If you are not impressive, they will not listen again. Even worse, they may tell others about their negative experience.

When notoriety sets in, remember to remain humble and grateful for the opportunity to perform and receive acknowledgement. In many cases your personality may get you further than your talent. There is a lot of talent in the world. The difference between you and them, could come down to likeability. No one wants to book an artist who is late for shows, has total disregard for the promoters request and basically does what he or she pleases with no concern of others.

When you arrive to your performance venue, be punctual. Don't extend your "**sound check**" past the allowed time. During sound checks, the artist gets onto the stage, check their microphones, musician's equipment, and monitor placement, then promptly get off stage to allow the flow of sound check to continue. The efficiency of your sound check is integral, as other artists may also need to execute a sound check prior to their performance.

Speaking to other artists and creating strong networks and professional relationships can benefit you in several ways. For example, building positive **rapport** with the sound engineer may enable him/her to ensure that your sound equipment is above average during your performance. When performing, be the person in which you are. In other words, be you! Easier said than done. I know. With practice, your comfort ability level on stage will improve.

Being natural and comfortable on stage, will get noticed and prompt return calls requesting you to perform again. Your fans expect you to be a "**star**". A star has more than just singing ability, many stars also have likeability. Fans appreciate a good show, and

an even better personality. Your listeners and fans like to feel as though you are singing to them directly. This connection is effective in many areas of on-stage performance.
Audience members need to feel as though there is a connection with the person on stage. The best way to create the audience connection is by singing songs which they can relate to.

Engage with the audience between songs instead of simply singing your song-list. Engaging with the audience, future and current fans consists of making them feel special and giving them the understanding that you appreciate their current and future support. Don't be afraid to express "**humility**". Give fans something to remember. You want to leave them wanting more.

Off Stage

Off stage appearances and performances can sometimes be a little tricky. There's a difficult balance of "star" appeal and "normalcy". This is the time when fans may get a glimpse into your natural personality. This is why remaining true to yourself is a requirement. It's hard to maintain a façade when speaking candidly.

For this section, off stage appearances will pertain to radio, in-person interviews, television, local events and normal outings. As you build your career and advance to a level where radio appearances are booked in advance, you must also learn what's expected from mainstream artists. Once you're scheduled to appear on radio, you need to relax! So many emotions and thoughts will begin to run through your mind: Do I wear this, who will be there, should I act like a star, etc.?

Actually, this is an opportunity to gain new followers and fans. When appearing for radio, always dress for the part. You are an artist, therefore, you should look like an artist. Dress for the person you aspire to be. Be aware that everyone has a camera, there may be photos taken of you. Always remain camera ready. When being interviewed, make sure that you are keeping the listeners focused on your music. Even if the conversation steers in another direction, be sure to plug in your music promotion.

Remain neutral on controversial topics. Don't discuss politics, religion, or voice your opinion on hot topics. Never speak negatively of other artists. If you're compared to another artist, focus on your uniqueness without being offensive to the other artist's achievements. If you're asked of your opinion, be sure to stay "middle of the road". Also, maintain confidentiality on your personal life. This is especially important if it has nothing to do with your music.

The music industry has many struggles in today's competitive environment. Artists speaking negatively about one another in order to make themselves appear more talented is compared to the "crabs in a barrel theory". Stay positive throughout your interview. Capitalize on your opportunity to gain new followers from your radio interview.

~

"There's enough success for everyone. Fans adore many artists. They have enough support to stay loyal to several artists at once."

~

Prior to your radio interview, research the person who will be interviewing you. Know something other than their name. Impress them, show them you're not just all about you, but you actually took the time to learn about them. This shows professionalism. Once you're done with your on-air interview, thank the station. No artist should ever go to a radio interview empty handed. Ensure that you have plenty of music to leave them.

    A television appearance can be very instrumental to your career. This is impressive on a one-sheet press release. Unlike a radio interview your fans not only get to hear you, but now they can see you. As you prepare for the TV appearance, days prior, make sure you do a similar research as the radio interviewer, familiarize yourself with the show host.

What type questions do they prefer to ask their artists? Don't go in there unprepared because it will definitely show. Know everything about your career. Make sure your manager has prompted and informed you of everything going on in your career. Unlike radio interviews, you won't be able to have a cheat sheet of all your upcoming shows and appearances. Depending on the interview purpose, familiarize yourself with everything pertaining to your music.

Your stylist should handle your fashion and wardrobe. Assure that your hair, makeup, and clothing has an official look. This gives the impression of an established and professional artist. During the interview, stay engaged with the host. Look as though you are excited to be there, but don't act as if this is your first ever interview. When speaking, look at the host. Avoid awkward camera stares while answering questions and especially wandering eyes. This could insinuate that you're untrustworthy, uncomfortable, or even lying! Study body language and interviewing skills.

As you begin to relay your message, be passionate. Be honest when discussing your music, your path, and when answering questions. Don't try to be believable, just be natural. Mistakes are going to happen. The good thing is that editing can fix those. Smile, when you can, and have fun!

Live Performances

The opportunity to perform live and on stage is considered the ultimate feeling of accomplishment by many artists. Live performances can be a challenge to many, but with practice and a new approach, it can become more natural, with time. In this section, we will discuss ways to improve your live performances.

As a young child, I still remember attending concerts where I was able to watch a variety of performers and their different styles. As I watched, I would observe their moves on stage, then go home to practice, in hopes of feeling and looking like a star. We all can be inspired and influenced by others. I suggest that you attend concerts of many different music genres.

While attending, observe ways in which the performer engages with the audience. What about their performance did you like? Did you not like? You don't want to copy their whole routine, but surely they must have a few key performance techniques which you can learn from? As you watch the performer, notice how they walk on stage after being introduced. Did he have a band, did she have an accompanying music track?

Be sure when you are given the opportunity to perform, that you are introduced to the audience with a lot of energy and excitement. If you have a band, prepare a musical intro. If you're performing **cover music**, sing something very popular. This gets the crowd engaged and on your side and its then up to you to mess it up!

After attending a few concerts, start rehearsing. Your rehearsal be held at an actual rehearsing studio with full mirrors. If a small stage is available that's an added bonus. As you rehearse, have a set list. By having a preset list of your songs to perform, you will have an opportunity to see your performance prior to the "live" show. Practice your set until you have perfected it. Once you have memorized your set and routines; continue adding elements to your show, such as short narratives in between songs that will take the audience on a short journey.

It's okay to practice while standing in front of the mirror. Memorizing stories and conversations which you would like to have with the audience is acceptable. There is no rule which states that you cannot have your conversations and stories memorized. This may change once you are performing live because no two audiences will be the same. As you are practicing, try new things on stage. This will give you a sense of your performance

www.GreenwaveEntertainment.com

style. Also, record your rehearsals with a video camera and watch at a later time. This enables you to see your performance just as an audience would.

Now you have rehearsed and you're ready for a live show. Start with a small venue. The last thing you want is to add more stress than necessary, by having a large crowd in which to entertain. Once you have been booked, be sure to invite all of your very close supporters. Having a supportive audience for your first performance will build your confidence.

~

"While you are on stage, listen for the feeling, the feeling which flows from you and ignites your passion."

~

While performing, be natural. Don't constantly think about your choreography. If you've practiced, the "moves" will feel and appear natural. Coming off as uncomfortable, will make your audience feel uncomfortable.

Move around the stage, don't stand in one spot. Listeners want an engaging live performance, something exhilarating.

When walking onto the stage, going directly to your microphone and singing, will get you nowhere. Whatever song you are singing know the song lyrics. When you rehearse read the song lyrics to yourself aloud, so you can really understand what message the song is relaying to the listener. It may call for facial expressions, eye contact, or maybe your own personal story.

Try to appear as if you have done this a million times. That's when you know you are in the right path and are flowing in your passion.

Social Media

Scroll any social media site and you will see the growing number of aspiring artists uploading new tunes, for their followers to hear. We see new posts to *Facebook*® walls, new songs uploaded to *sound cloud*® and *YouTube*® videos. We also can't help but notice the social media posts uploaded by these artist in attempt to build their fan base.

Social media is an avenue used to stay connected to artist and observe their personality and lives when off-stage. Artists utilize these resources as a tool in which they can build a solid fan base. This tool can also introduce your music to parts of the world, where otherwise, they would have not been exposed. Just as television and radio, social media posts also must censored. Social media can ruin a major portion of your career with one "unacceptable" or negative post.

Most major artists have publicist who post onto social media on their behalf. But as a new artist, you typically will be in charge of your own posts.

As you begin to post, don't flood your page with just your music. Give a variety of interesting topics that can catch the attention of all people. If you only post your music, then people become bored and no longer interested. Keep in mind that followers and fans like to feel connected. If they feel as though they "know" you, they are more likely to support your projects

As you continue posting updates, remember to be limited on information about your personal life and your views on controversial topics. Artists should use good discernment when deciding what to upload to the internet. We want everyone to hear your new song, or latest performance video, but remember, if it's not the best representation of you, don't upload it. You have to be mindful of what you're uploading. An mp3 recorded with a handheld recorder will typically have bad sound quality. Bad sound quality could do more damage than help when attempting to impress followers.

When someone stumbles upon your page, they should first encounter professional photos. If you publish candid photos of yourself, ensure they are clear and appropriate. Update your status regularly. Use social media as a way to interact with friends,

www.GreenwaveEntertainment.com

new fans, and family. Don't simply post just to post, interact with others. Social media is the most popular way to grow a fan base, so don't miss out on a free marketing tool which could advance your career to the next level.

Chapter 3 Music Selection

You may have heard the saying: "That song is perfect for that singer". Well that can be true for you as well. Basically, the artist or their management team has selected the best songs which highlights the artist talents. This often occurs through a lengthy, tedious selection process. But there are times when it transpires via "pure luck" and instantaneously. Let's discuss this further.

As an artist, live performances can alter a new or veteran musician's career. This is the moment where raw talent or extensive rehearsal is showcased. There's no Auto Tune or software which can correct any mistakes during a live performance. This is your moment as an artist to reveal your true talent. When you and your team decide to select the songs in which you are to perform, you have to be sure of a few things important aspects.

First, you must decide if your song selection is appropriate for your live performance. All great singers are not great when singing certain songs. Whitney Houston's song, "I Will Always Love you" is a song created specifically for her and her singing abilities. She maintained the perfect tone and pitch for the song. She understood how to sing the song. She allowed the song to sing through her, meaning the song took over her as she performed it live. It was almost as if she was the song. As many times as this song has been performed by other artists, no one was able to perform it as Whitney. It was her perfect song.

So you too have to find that perfect to perform. The lyrical content must mean so much to you that you lose yourself when singing the words. When selecting songs to perform during your next live event, be sure to select songs which enhance your signing abilities. Don't focus strictly on what the audience may want to hear, but concentrate on the strongest selection for your voice. Imagine Whitney Houston singing a Beyonce song. This would have a different affect to the listeners and the impact of her talent may have been compromised. Ask yourself these questions: Do I have to change my style completely for this song? Am I singing the song comfortably? Does this song take away from my vocal ability?

You have qualities as an artist which makes you unique. Find the song which feels natural. Avoid songs that may require you to transform into another artist. There have been Christian artists who are able to perform to non-Christian audiences successfully. This is due to the artists selecting songs which were a "value-add" to their voice ability. They were comfortable with the song, and that allowed the audience to become engaged.

Another major question: Do you love the song, or just like it? This is important as while you're on stage; your love, or despair, for the song will show. If you are in love with the song, the audience will react positively. Very few things can be hidden while performing live. If you just "like" the song, the audience may pick up on your lack of enthusiasm. The audience wants to hear you perform a song in which you love!

   If you are preparing to start recording songs for an upcoming album or **Extended Play** (EP); song choices are very important too. Similarly, when selecting songs for your album be sure they represent you as the artist. Be sure they are true to your vocal abilities and persona. This is the time when a professional producer should be utilized. Every song which you have recorded does not necessarily have to be included on your album. You must remember to select songs which captivates the listeners. When selecting songs for the album they should inspire or move you, personally. If the song seems dry to you, it will also seem dry to listeners. You and your producer should absolutely love the selections.

www.GreenwaveEntertainment.com

While listening to the songs and editing for hours in the studio, the selected songs should still move you. If you bore of a song, the listeners will tire much more quickly. As you select your songs and have found songs that you enjoy listening to and performing, it's time to test the waters and let a few friends listen. Be careful with this, some friends are such great friends, so that anything you produce, they will enjoy. Because of this, we must find the honest friends, friends who know music and aren't afraid to tell you: "I didn't really like this song".

If you get a review from your friend or producer friend which doesn't sit well with you, it's okay. Constructive criticism has its place in the studio and music industry. This doesn't mean you are going to trash the song, but it gives you and the producer aspects of your music to observe. There may be something you may not have considered while producing the song. That one minor correction could change the entirety of the song. There have been minor word changes or one chord change which helped create a hit song. I have also found it very helpful to let a child or an older adult listen to the song. When a kid hears a song that they like, they will remember it. A song doesn't need to be complicated. The key is for the song to be retained after listening for first time. A child or an elderly person may be the most honest in regards to the song quality. Do they remember anything from the song? Did they like the song? And if so, you may have you a great song for your album.

Production

In a world of "fly by night" producers and a variety of sound engineering software, readily accessible. Finding a reputable producer can be challenging. As a new artist, in the entertainment industry, finally hearing your song recorded, may feel like the world. But this is where it all begins. Once your song has been recorded successfully, the next important part is post production.

Once you have completed recording, there will editing needed for the vocals. When searching for a vocal editor, ensure they are reputable. Ask to listen to their most recent work. Compare it to your favorite songs heard on the radio. Once you're convinced you have selected the best audio engineer, move forward. The next step is your mix and mastering.

Mix and mastering is very important and can be just as expensive as the recording. If you listen to an unmixed song, it will sound very small and compact, as if all the sounds are basically on top of each other. An accurate mix should sound wide to your ears. Sound clarity and balance should be heard throughout. Once your song is mixed and mastered, compare it to your favorite song on the radio. There should be little to no difference in sound quality.

Listen to your newly recorded song on several different audio devices, computer speakers, car speakers, and studio speakers.

www.GreenwaveEntertainment.com

The quality should all be the same. If there is a noticeable difference in sound quality, you may need to consider hiring a different audio engineer! Production can make a positive or negative impact on a song. If your song is an "easy-listen", then your listeners may not have a problem focusing on the song itself versus the obvious production issues. In conclusion, be sure your audio engineer is someone who can provide your music the best quality possible!

Radio

Radio play is considered a high achievement for many new artists. There is no secret formula which guarantees radio play, but let's cover a few things that will definitely help.

Radio is a business that is controlled by listeners. Listeners have a huge say in which songs will actually be played or continue to be played on radio. Because listeners decide what will be played as well as how often, by their requests; you will need to market your music in area where your listeners are concentrated. Go where your fans are, so they can hear your new song. Getting your fan base behind you and your new song is a major way to obtain exposure on radio stations. When performing live, don't simply ask the listeners to purchase your cd from your cd booth, ask them to call their local radio and request the song to be played! Radio responds to listener's persistent request.

Radio does require a budget. This budget is used for **Radio Promotion**, or a Radio Campaign. The purpose of the radio campaign is to introduce your music to radio and to influence the program directors that it's a song which they should add to rotation. Radio promoters should have a working relationship with Radio Program Directors (PD). Program directors are in charge of adding new music to the radio's playlist rotation. You want to select a radio promoter who has a strong working relationships with program directors from all markets. The promoter will contact the program director and introduce you, the artist, and your song. Once the song is submitted to the program director the promoter should contact them weekly in order to retrieve any feedback they can from the PD.

The radio promoter will acknowledge if the PD has had an opportunity to hear the artist's song. All songs are not going to be accepted and this could be based on the season. As spring and summer arrives, more upbeat, high energy will control the airwaves. As the season changes and fall arrives, the songs tend to slow down. There will remain a few upbeat songs, but your great ballads will begin to emerge. No matter the genre, holiday songs will dominate radio airwaves beginning in late November and all of December.

No new artist should release new music during this time unless it's Christmas music. Your music will be overlooked, ignored, placed on a shelf and possibly never heard of again. This can be a costly mistake! When you begin to market your music to radio stations, do not forget about the secondary stations. These are stations that do not report to Billboards for charting purposes. These stations receive high listenership. Secondary stations increase the likelihood of getting a good quality song some airtime. Program directors for these stations are not as selective as your Billboard Radio one stations.

In the 21st century internet radio has advanced and plays an integral role in the music industry. Don't be afraid to market your music to internet radio. Internet radio can be streamed anywhere and anytime of day. Remember radio isn't about popularity of its stations, but more about getting your song heard! Listeners may hear your song while on the internet at work and they may even take the time to purchase it from a digital music store, if it's available. Additionally, never market a song to radio prior to uploading the song to a digital music store.

www.GreenwaveEntertainment.com

Internet radio has stations in every part of the world, with very few to no limitations. Gaining popularity on internet radio could open the opportunity for possible gigs and appearances. Now that you have begun to get noticed on the radio, you should begin constructing your radio tour. This means you will begin contacting radio stations to request an interview. This is an important role for an artist.

Your listeners would love to hear from you. Start off by interviewing regionally. Select a region and saturate their radio market. As you set up these interviews, be sure that you show your appreciation to the program director. Gift cards and cd's are a great way to show the station your appreciation. Another added bonus is to sponsor an event hosted by the station. By becoming a sponsor, this shows that you're not only concerned with marketing your music to the program director, but you actually want to build a relationship with the station.

~

"Radio is very important, but don't be discouraged if your first song released is not considered a "hit".

~

Some stations will play a song and if it may not fit well with their current line-up. Regardless of how great the song may be, they may pass and select another song that's a better fit. Keep pushing, keep contacting and if your song is a hit, someone will notice and give you radio opportunity!

Getting Your Fans Involved

In order for your career to grow, you will need fans. A person who believes in you, will purchase tickets to your performances or buy your records. Let's discuss the importance of involving your fans.

As stated earlier in this book, social media can be an easy and cost-efficient avenue for artist to reach their fans. Stay active on your social media sites. Get your fans

www.GreenwaveEntertainment.com

involved with the process. Ask questions, involve them in the process, such as selecting the new cd cover, new songs to add to your next set list. Once again, fans want to feel as if they get a behind the scenes look into your music making. As you are in the studio writing or recording music, be sure to capture those moments on video or at least photos. Upload these images and tell your fans about the process. Don't tell all but give your fans some information to keep them interested. Also don't be afraid to comment and interact with your fans.

Fans can really get to know an artist at a live performance. During your show make sure you are involved with the fans. Depending on the size of the concert, you can get your fans involved by asking the audience for song requests, as long as you have a very versatile band. Be cautious to sing songs that you know you can actually sing and that represent who you are as an artist. Stay in your genre. As you are on stage give a ways are always a great way to get fans on your side. As you are performing throughout your set, take a break and ask your audience questions about your music or about something that relates to music. The audience member with the correct answer gets a free copy of your cd or tickets to your next show. Help your audience feel special. Fan or crowd participation helps familiarize those who may not know you. It also helps them to remember you. So get them as involved as possible while you're on stage.

As stated previously in the Radio section, giveaways to the station are very good method used to show the station your appreciation for considering. Moreover, with radio you can also interact with the listening audience. Even if you don't have an interview for your music, take any and all opportunities to give prized to station listeners on behalf of your name. With the holidays, there's a lot of families who will go without their basic necessities during the holiday season. This is a perfect opportunity to give back to your community.

Contact the station of your choice and offer to give turkeys for Thanksgiving, toys for Christmas time, or volunteer your time to less fortunate families during the holiday season. Do this with an open heart and a giving spirit. Nothing looks better for a new artist than wanting to create a positive image by giving back to their community. This is a well-respected act and will gain much attention. I have also experienced artists who gives prizes of gift cards, gas cards, or some artist apparel through radio stations, for no particular reason other than community service. Be creative with your ideas and try to involve your current and future fans!

Song Promotion

Promotion of your newly released song is very important. In the music industry, there are professionals who help with promoting your music so you can better focus on your craft. When promoting music, there are many areas of focus. Once you determine your target audience you can now begin promoting. We have discussed social media and radio as promotional avenues, but there are new and innovative ways to reach the masses. As you hire your promoter, make sure that they able to market as well.

New Artist approach to music promotion is different than artists who are signed to major record labels. The most important aspect is the ability to be smart about the money in which you are planning to spend on marketing and promotion. With a tight budget, as most independent artist typically start with, it is very vital to know which songs are unlikely to gain major exposure. Another tough feat is the ability to realistically gauge potential sales and releases suitably.

Dependent upon some luck and talent some albums you release may or may not sell enough to support spending thousands of dollars for marketing and promotion. If you have a hit song, your producer and music executives have listened and believe you have a great song. Take a chance on yourself and invest the money for the proper marketing and promotion, this could be your big break!

Every artist should have a **Press Release** when preparing to release an album. Your press release is your promotional campaign information card. If you are going to create your own or have one professionally developed for you, here are a few things to keep in mind: First, keep it short and sweet. Another name for your press release is **One Sheet**. Which means all of your information is placed on One Sheet of paper. Even though you may feel as though every minute detail pertaining to your career isn't there. It's better to lean more on the short side than to compose the press release which is too long. Just include your career highlights and current projects!

On the backside of the press release include all of the relevant information a journalist would need to perform a write-up in regards to current and future promotions without directly speaking to you. Therefore, when developing your Press Release, be mindful that the written speech of your press release should be similar to writing a news story. Include information about yourself, your music, background and future. Be sure to remember that you should leave the door open for a member of the media to contact you for more info or to set up an interview.

As a new or experienced artist you may not have an established relationship with members of the media. Therefore, you shouldn't automatically expect your phone to start ringing as soon as your music arrives. Typically, you will need to follow-up a few times to get a response. But don't fret; it's okay. This doesn't mean you've done something wrong in promoting your music. That's typical of the industry, and the next time as you continue promoting, it will be much easier. Settle into the possibly that responses are unlikely to be

www.GreenwaveEntertainment.com

prompt. Successful campaigns may take time, but don't give up, stay the course.

Chapter 4 Growth

~

"Problem/desire identified, steps necessary to overcome, obstacles faced, now it's time to revel in the joy."

~

You are not only an artist, but a recording artist. Turning your passion into a career may be your next goal. Many albums and songs are released daily, nationally and globally. So you may be wondering, "How do I begin to make a mark in the industry, as a newcomer?" This is where great coaching comes into play.

As you start your new career you may face many unexpected challenges and obstacles along the way. The first challenge is: getting booked! Selling CD's, digitally or physically, is not the primary avenue of revenue for artists. Artists, signed or unsigned, earn a majority of their income from tours and concerts. Getting booked on a tour takes hard work, dedication, and networking.

This is a goal which some veteran artists are still trying to achieve. Promoters may reach out to you, due to general recognition. Or your management team must work hard to connect with these promoters in order to get you booked. Artists tend to find this task difficult. As you begin to discuss this with your manager or band, be sure to remember that all artists were once new.

Depending on your music genre, you may have to begin to attend places where your genre is played live. As you attend these events or concerts, find out about the promoter. The purpose of knowing who is in charge is to earn an introduction. Even if you don't have a "team" per se, use a friend or anyone besides yourself. You may automatically gain more respect when you don't speak for yourself. Executives tend to frown upon self-promotion; it can seem as if you're a little self absorbed. Once you know the promoter, have your manager speak for you, smile, show interest and remain open.

At this point you are looking to get booked not to pay your car note. You are seeking an opening opportunity, or a few minutes to showcase your talent. You basically want to get one foot in the door at this time. Keep in mind this gig may not pay anything and you may end up investing your own money for your first few events. This builds your live performance resume and earns respect from the promoter who also has contact with other promoters. Once you get this gig, you are responsible for impressing the audience and promoter. Follow the guidelines we discussed earlier in this book regarding your live performance instructions about punctuality, etc.

Selling your music can be another obstacle. As you review chapter 3, which discusses marketing, you must understand that every artist will sell and market differently. Great sales are accomplished by great music and marketing. If no one knows your music

www.GreenwaveEntertainment.com

exists, then they can't purchase it. There used to be days when artists desired to have their music sold in stores. Today, artists are able to upload their new music to digital stores for less than $20.00. And with the right marketing strategy, anyone can make an unnumbered amount of sales. As a new artist setting a record sales goal will help you stay on track with your marketing plan.

When you prepare to release music always start off with a single. Singles give your followers a chance to hear and learn a song without much investment. Releasing a full album prior to releasing a single normally results in poor sales. A great single builds anticipation for the full album. So when you prepare to release your single, I suggest you start your goal with selling 100 CD's. Understandably, 100 sales may not sound like a big goal, but keep in mind, with the economy shift people are very focused on how they spend their money.

Anyone who decides to spend $0.99 on a music download from a relatively unknown artist is an accomplishment! I'm sure you can think of 100 family and close friends who would love to support your new music and your goal of becoming a professional musician. As long as you take the proper steps mentioned in the previous chapters regarding your vocal work and image branding, your music should catch their attention and possibly lead to more word of mouth promoting by them. Word of mouth can be your best seller. In the past, well-known artists have released self titled album with no typical marketing plan. The surprise release of their album was solely spread by word of mouth, which one in particular sold 828,773 copies in just 3 days, making it the fastest selling album, ever.

As you begin to market, never rule out the old-school word of mouth. It can catch on like wildfire. As you sell your first 100 CD's revel in joy! That is a big deal. Keep pushing and promoting. Continue building your team, as a great addition. The more people you have talking about your music, the more you have wanting to buy your music. Ask for supporters who purchase your music to post their comments about the newly released single. Reviews are what the world is counting on. A 5 star rating will catch a consumer's attention and prompt them to at least look at the product. Build a great team of individuals who don't mind spreading the word about your new single. Don't stop until you reach your goal. You can do it!

Why is the hard work worth it?

The life of a mainstream music artist is not one to be taken as an easy road to stardom. As we watch TV mesmerized by the celebrity status, the big houses and fancy cars, it's easy to think "Wow they wrote a song and now they're rich." It's not quite that simple.

Most artists have dreams of becoming a singer who travels all over the world to perform in front of screaming fans who know every word of their song. Dreams are possible to anyone who believes, and also has the work ethic to make it happen.

~

"Nothing in life will ever be given to you and enjoyed the way you enjoy accomplishing it with your hard work".

~

The music industry is no different. Artists must not chase the dream of becoming a mainstream artist with the work ethic of someone who is not dedicated. The art of becoming a great singer can be instilled as a child, but there is work you must do. A majority of nationally recognized singers all across the world who have made music their career do have a special gift to sing and perform, but talent without work doesn't create a great artist. As you have read through the guide, you may have noticed that this industry requires a lot from you - from image branding to stylist, to a great rehearsal routine.

This is only the beginning to making it mainstream. I am a coach and I push people to be great, but you will never get there if you don't have sleepless nights and early mornings due to that fact you are working on you talent. This career is for the strong at heart, those who know that it's not easy, but it is possible. Let me be the first to tell you that becoming a millionaire in the music industry is by far one of the hardest things to accomplish. If you do this because you love it, one, it will never feel like work, and two, you won't need money to verify that you are doing what you love.

      Hard work has to be understood in order to succeed. Don't talk yourself out of the journey ahead of you. You will have ups and downs, you will spend a lot of money, and people will say things you won't like. Use those influences for your fuel to go harder! Close your ears to negative people, or those who may not believe in what you are doing. Keep a positive mind, at all times. When things get hard, think of why you chose to become a singer.

---

www.GreenwaveEntertainment.com

Your hard work will pay off. Those who dedicate themselves to push further than what they can see today, will see success. All success is not measured the same. Some artist would like to see their song on *itunes®* for sale, while others are looking to one day sing on the stage of the *MTV Awards®*. Whatever your goal, stick to it. However, it will take work. Not only hard work in the studio, but it will take an open mind, which can be hard work. You are an artist and it sometimes takes someone else to tell you how to make your art "better". Remain open, and always remember you were given 2 ears and one mouth. This means to always listen more than you speak. The more you listen to those in which you have entrusted with your career growth, the better chance you will have in succeeding and progressing.

Singing should be the first thing on your mind in the morning and the last thing before you go to bed. The only way to succeed is to study your craft. If you are keen to those in your industry who are succeeding, you too can succeed. Study their success. It's ok to ask questions. If you don't know something that's ok too, being honest with yourself and your abilities will lead to you growing as an artist. You can now work on improving your weaknesses. Use this guide book, but also use other sources to grow your gift.

Read a lot of books about the industry. There are so many sources to help you grow as an artist. But like I have stated over and over, in this book, it is going to take a lot of hard work. Just know what you put in, you will get out of it. If you sew hard work and sweat, you will reap a great harvest in your career. No matter the obstacle, keep pushing, work harder and don't look for a quick turn around, be patient. Keep your mind focused on working hard to perfect the gift and talent you possess.

Don't get off track by focusing on the gilts and glam of the industry. That's only a small percentage of what singing as a professional provides. Undoubtedly, know that

www.GreenwaveEntertainment.com

you were called to do this and let no obstruction stop you from achieving greatness. The joys of becoming a professional singer will begin to sink in as you work hard. It is then where you can reflect and see the accomplishments of your hard work. This should only elevate you to a greater level. Even when you have toured the world, there is still greatness for you to accomplish. Stay focused on your goal and go after it with everything you have within. 1000 no's to 1 yes can change your career and catapult you to a new dimension in your career. Work hard and never give up. Your goal is obtainable.

What to expect next?

Next, you are now ready to get busy! You have read the chapters and now it's time to put what you have learned to work. These chapters are created for artists who have an open mind to coaching.

Nothing great is built in one day, but does have a start day. So today must be your day to start toward a great career in music.

www.GreenwaveEntertainment.com

Expect to work very hard, and for those who have been in music for years, you may even have to begin to forget those things you were taught in the beginning. Everything you have learned in the past was to get you to that next point in your career.

You will eventually begin to build a great fan-base of those who know your music. If you stick to the steps and can continue to put out a great product, it will be acknowledged. As your fans increase, don't let it distract you from being a great person. Nothing hurts a career more than an artist who doesn't recognize their fans and feels they have already "made it". Music is constantly changing, so as an artist, stay loyal to your fans and stay current with the industry. This industry is extremely competitive and sometimes cut throat. Many people will not make it to mainstream, many will. Expect nothing but greatness as you are moving forward in every step of your career.

Once you have become an independent artist and you have released your own music, sales are good, and radio spins have picked up, you should have began to chart on billboards. Your sound-scan report should look great and then record labels will begin to seek a recording contract with you. Labels want an artist that understands the industry, in which you are now apart of, and an artist who has had some success on their own. Use this guide book in a way to get comfortable with what industry executives are looking for in an artist. Becoming a signed artist can be a great reward because most of the recording, marketing and radio work will then be their responsibility.

    Now you, the artist, are able to strictly focus on singing and recording. But, again, in order for the artist to gain the attention, you will need to be polished and understand the industry. Labels will sometimes sign new artist to a one-album contract with the possibility of an extension, depending on the success of the first album. Record labels put a lot of work and money into artists and will have high standards and expectations. Many artist signed to record labels are dropped because they do not sell enough records. This is just the way it goes.

A record company may spend $1 million on the artist from production to marketing, including an artist cash advance. An advance is money given to the artist to cover recording and music videos to give the artist creative control. But this money at the end of the day has to be recouped by the record label before the artist ever sees any money from sales of their albums. Being signed to a record label can be the greatest thing for some and not so much for others.

As an independent artist, you will notice it takes a budget to get top quality work completed. Therefore, artists may raise money by starting funds or having car washes or anything that can help their band raise enough funds to cover those services. But when you finally raise that money, you are able to get the services you need. Even though you may not have a large budget, as a major label, you can still do great in comparison to the amount of

www.GreenwaveEntertainment.com

albums you will need to sell to break even and start earning income. Being signed to a label; a lot of these services are already provided.

Clothing, travel, and radio expenses may be covered by the record label in which an artist is signed. You will also typically sell more albums being signed to the major label. But you will definitely have a higher amount of albums you will need to sell in order to obtain a profit. So both are great, but understand it will take work either way. You may not consider being signed to a record, but whatever your choice, be certain that you are well-informed. If it's something in which you may not be familiar with, learn it.

Physical endurance is a topic which was not discussed earlier. After you begin with the rehearsal chapter of this book, you will notice the amount of rehearsal practice required. As a professional singer you should be in your best shape. Getting physically fit should be another step in your process. Getting in shape doesn't mean go on a strict diet, but as a singer you must be cautious of things you eat. Foods, such as: dairy products and cold drinks, being ingested before a performance, is an example of a restriction. Keep in mind that you may have to begin cardio workouts. Cardio workouts are always beneficial for your body and your voice.

Raising your heart rate at least once a day is also helpful. Being in top fitness and performing without interruption is desirable for the audience and promoter. Keep in mind that health and fitness is a part of mainstream singing. It is ideal if you are able to get a professional trainer, but if not, at least see your doctor and get a physical examination. Allow a professional to give you medical advice and guide you in the right direction. Great things are sure to come to those who work hard. Expect greatness!

Where would you be without this guidebook?

Years ago when I entered into the music industry and began coaching artists, I

www.GreenwaveEntertainment.com

discovered there was a need for a "how-to guide". A guide which assists artist understand what is takes to be successful. The information in this book is from my professional experiences over years.

Without a guide, artists may feel like a traveler without a map, guessing for the right direction. So my purpose is to help artists find their destination, by using this guidebook. With this book, I want you to gain the courage you may need to go further and expose you to additional information. Often, artists do not go beyond their comfort zone.

Without this guide book, where would you be? You would still be doing music as before and possibly steering your career into the wrong direction. Without this guide book, your understanding to the music industry could be tainted by the façade's impersonated in mass media. You now understand what it takes in becoming a great artist. This guidebook has given you step by step directions to get started in the right direction. No longer do you have to wonder if you should be looking for a vocal producer to help you in your studio session, you have learned that having a vocal producer can be one of the most important parts to recording in the studio.

You have also learned how to use social media to spread the word of your new music release. No longer should you guess what to post on social media websites. As we discussed in the social media section, knowing what to post can help your career. Because of this guide book you are now a step closer to your dream.

It's going to take a lot of work in a very competitive industry, but you are able to beat the odds more effectively with coaching and guidance. The knowledge you have gained from this guide book and by following the instructions, will help you at any level or stage of your career. Even if you are recording your own album, signed to a label, or just singing for fun; this guide book has information to help you succeed. I have seen the information from this

www.GreenwaveEntertainment.com

guide book help people. I have coached new artists, not knowing anything, to now knowing a great deal of information that has helped them and will continue to help them for years to come.

I hope this book helped you realize that you too are special. You have an "it" factor, which is unique. You should use that to stand apart from every other artist. Never strive to be just like the next singer. Even if that singer has made millions, fans do not want to see a replica of their favorite artist.

Fans love to learn of new artists and see their special characteristics, which set them apart from everyone else. That is what intrigues them into buying your music. There is no way to compete with someone being who is being themselves. You can't be a better version of someone else. Therefore be you, love you and cultivate your gift.

You have also leaned that image is very important. Find people who specialize in the services that you need. It's ok to say, "I don't

www.GreenwaveEntertainment.com

do that, but he/she does". This is a trait which makes great leaders. They understand that they are not experts in each area and have perfected the art of delegation. **Delegating** someone with more expertise in an area to help you is intelligent and asking for help sometimes requires a strong person. Be confident, in yourself, to know that you're ok with someone else taking your image ideas and suggesting additional options for a more professional appearance. After all, the entire goal is to be great and it all begins with your image.

Take the knowledge which you've learned here, and catapult your career. Impress radio personalities in your interview by knowing more about the hosts than they would expect you to know. Use every bit of information that you can and let it leave impressions in the music industry. You are great with or without this book, but now you are going to be great while taking your career into the right direction and enhancing your talents.

People will begin to look at you differently. They will realize that you have taken you career serious. This will only lead to more CD sales and support. There is nothing better than growing your career because of the hard work you invested, instead of seeking handouts. Take control of your career and don't let it start without any guidance. You are in control and you hold the reigns, so guide it with this guide book, I wrote just for you. Guide it and you will be rewarded by your hard work.

Chapter 5 Conclusion

Can you answer these questions?

- *Singing in front of large crowds, hearing your music on the radio, and touring the country is your desire?*
- *You want to be a nationally recognized artist?*
- *Tell me, how do you intend to get there?*
- *What steps do you take, what producers will you use, what image do you want to portray?*

www.GreenwaveEntertainment.com

- *What is your first step?*

All of these questions, and more, were discussed throughout this guide. My job, as a coach, is to ensure that when you are done with this book, you could answer these questions.

There will be many obstacles that come after and during each step of the way, but you now own a guide which can be used, at anytime, to review the necessary steps to help you over a rough patch. I have made certain to include problem areas and solutions that are most commonly encountered during the beginning stages of a music career. It is nearly impossible to address each and every aspect or issue in which you may encounter on your journey, but the most common facets are discussed.

Your Next Steps

Assuming you have read straight through this book, I'm requesting that you go back to the beginning. You will now use this

www.GreenwaveEntertainment.com

book as a guide. You want to go step by step with each section and chapter. Analyze your career; know where you are currently and where you are headed. Be honest with yourself. Don't give yourself any leverage; take it for what it is.

If you know you need to work on your vocals, work on your vocals and get them right. Don't just go into this career of music with only the blessings of mom and dad. You will need training. No matter what career you chose, there has to be some formal training. Training will only enhance your gift. Don't let it lower your self-confidence; consider it as an additional tool to sharpen your skills. Elevate yourself to a new level by doing what the professionals do, train!

If you have already recorded your record and received positive feedback from peers and producers, analyze your image. Where did your current image originate? Were your image ideas by accident, or did you hire a professional stylist? Let your professional

www.GreenwaveEntertainment.com

stylist listen to your song; let them read the song lyrics. The purpose is so the stylist will have a better understanding of what you are trying to portray and your target audience. Your image and music has to coincide with one another. If you don't have the money, wait, save up and get the money so you can get the stylist. An important factor about good music is there is no time limit.

Songs recorded 20 years ago are still played on the radio today and sang all over the world for karaoke. So don't be discouraged if you happen to get to a step that may cost more money than you have at that moment. If your music is great today, it will be great tomorrow as well. Don't allow money as the reason your career never got off the ground. If you have to do "little by little", that's okay, as long as every step you take you are doing it at its highest potential.

You may have your image completed; your new music recorded and an upcoming release of your album. Reflect on all of your hard work. The sweat and tears that went into your creation. Do you want to just release your music for family and friends, or do you want as many people as possible to experience your new music? Of course we want the world to hear it. So you must hire a radio promoter, a liaison between you and the radio stations program director.

These promoters are sometimes expensive to obtain, but as previously stated, if you don't have the money right now, wait until you have the financing. Having a promoter doesn't automatically guarantee you radio plays, but not having a promoter at all, guarantees you zero radio play. Require your promoter to work your song for at least 6 month, consistently. Mail your CD's to stations for giveaways. Provide gift certificates to radio personnel to show your appreciation for the consideration of placing your new song in rotation.

You're ready now, you can do it! You have the knowledge to elevate your career to its next level. It's all up to you, how bad do you want it? Are you willing to give everything for your career? Are you willing to follow this guide and let the world experience you and your music at its highest quality? If yes, then I expect you to take every part of this book, dissect it and get a detailed understanding of every thing discussed. One last bit of advice, in this industry you will have to take chances. Record labels take chances on artists and radio stations takes chances on songs. You, as an artist, will have to take chances in your career. You may not always understand everything there is to know, but take a chance for the best and good will come from it. You may not always succeed at the speed you expected to, but if you stay true to your craft and work hard, good has to come your way. Stay focused, try hard, and if you fall, get up and try it again. Your hit song may be one song away. Keep rocking!

Glossary of Terms

Definitions

Behind the scenes - (*theater*) Behind the scenery and stage area; backstage. In secret; out of public view.

Branding - associate a product or service with a trademark or other name and related images.

Choreography- art of creating, arranging and recording the **dance movements of a ballet** etc

Cover song - version of a song that is a rerecording of that song

Demo - recording of a song meant to demonstrate its overall sound for the purpose of getting it published or recorded more full

Diction - effectiveness and degree of clarity of word choice, and presentation of said words.

Digital Download - the processing of copying data to a computer from an external source

www.GreenwaveEntertainment.com

Extended Play (EP) - musical recording that contains more music than a single, but is usually too short to qualify as a full studio album or LP

Graphic designer - a professional within the graphic design and graphic arts industry who assembles together images, typography, or motion graphics to create a piece of design

Humility - variously seen as the act or posture of lowering oneself in relation to others, or conversely, having a clear perspective, and therefore respect, for one's place in context

Image consultant - Fashion design is the art of the application of design and aesthetics or natural beauty to clothing and accessories. Fashion design is influenced by cultural and social latitudes, and has varied over time and place.

Music Executive - a person within a record label who works in senior management, making executive decisions in relation to the label's artists. Their role varies greatly but in essence, they can oversee one, or many, aspects of a record label, including A&R, contracts, management, publishing, production manufacturing, marking/promotion, distribution, copyright, and touring.

Official Marketing Materials - all sales promotional, marketing or
advertising materials produced or distributed by or on behalf of the Provider in connection with the Services or which otherwise make reference to the services

One Sheet - In the entertainment industry, a one-sheet or one sheet is a single document that summarizes a product for publicity and sales.

www.GreenwaveEntertainment.com

Portfolio - a range of investments held by a person or organization.

Press Release - a written or recorded communication directed at members of the news media for the purpose of announcing something ostensibly newsworthy

Program Director - the person who develops or selects some or all of the content that will be broadcast. A program director's selections are based upon expertise in the media as well as knowledge of the target demographic. Typically, a program director decides which radio or TV program will broadcast.

Rapport - occurs when two or more people feel that they are *in sync* or *on the same wavelength* because they feel similar or relate well to each other. Rapport is theorized to include three behavioral components: mutual attention, mutual positivity, and coordination.

Social media - the social interaction among people in which they create, share or exchange information and ideas in virtual communities and networks.

Sound check - the preparation that takes place before a concert, speech, or similar performance, when the performer and the sound crew run through a small portion of the upcoming show on the venue's sound system to make sure that the sound in the venue's "Front Of House" (FOH) and stage monitor sound systems is clear and at the right volume and tonal frequencies. Sound checks are especially important for popular and other musical genres that use heavily amplified PA systems; having correct sound is crucial to the success of such events.

Star - a term used to refer to a person who has great popular appeal and is widely known, prominence or success in a field.

www.GreenwaveEntertainment.com

www.GreenwaveEntertainment.com

Artists Checklists

Album Checklist

I. MAKING THE ALBUM

    A. PRE-RECORDING and PLANNING STEPS

        1. Decide what you're making: one album or an album series?

        2. Choose your songs

        3. Record at home or at a professional studio?

        4. Rehearse

        5. Fine tune your gear and instruments

    B. RECORDING STEPS

        1. Make mixes, listen, get feedback, and repeat

        2. Make final mixes

    C. MASTERING and POST-PRODUCTION STEPS

        1. Choose a mastering house

www.GreenwaveEntertainment.com

    2. Have the right formats and ask what files they need
    3. Decide the order of the songs on the album
    4. Decide on the amount of "space" between songs

D. LEGAL STEPS
    1. Document who owns the songs and sound recordings
    2. Get permission to record any cover songs, samples, or loops
    3. Clear the legal status of all the artwork
    4. Clear the legal status of all the text
    5. Get permission for guest musicians (if needed)

E. REPLICATION and DIGITAL DISTRIBUTION STEPS
    1. Replicating and duplicating CDs
        a. Determine how many CDs to make and the costs

       b. Decide on type of packaging (jewel case, sleeve, etc.) and what type of booklet (1 panel, 2 panel, multi-panel)

       c. Get artwork design templates from the CD Manufacturer or use their online design services

       d. Determine formats required for album art and text, CD art and text, etc., and use this format

  2. Print your own discs

  3. Digital Download Cards

F. ARTWORK and DESIGN

  1. Choose a name for the album

  2. Get a UPC barcode

  3. Work on the artwork

  4. Replicate the CD

       a. Send/Mail the mastered album along with artwork

       b. Proof artwork

           c. Sign copyright release and grant approval

II. PREPARING FOR THE ALBUM RELEASE
    A. Pick a Release Date

    B. Prepare for online sales

1. Select your Digital or CD Distributor and sign up

2. Create your album profile and upload artwork

    C. Plan your CD Release Show, Listening Party, and Tours

    D. Get Your Album Merchandise and Promotional Material

1. T-shirts, postcards, stickers, flyers

    E. Plan and Prepare the Publicity Campaign

        1. Set up a tracking system

        2. Send out your CDs, MP3s, and press releases

        3. Put up posters and flyers

        4. Follow up

        5. Update your "Music Resume" documents (Part II)

III. THE ALBUM RELEASE and POST-RELEASE

    A. Submit CD's for online sales
    B. Add your CD to pertinent release sites
    C. Legal
    D. Update your website and social media

Rehearsal Checklist

__Be prepared

__Have a rehearsal itinerary

__Have musicians to arrive 20 minutes before rehearsal to set up and warm up

__Set up microphones

__Set the placement of singers

__Singers arrive

__Open with prayer or some type of inspiration of why we have come together and announcements

__Singers and musicians warm up on 2 songs

__Start rehearsing your set

__Make sure that each vocal section and auxiliary knows their part

www.GreenwaveEntertainment.com

__Complete the set rehearsal
__Give singers and musicians instruction on what to work and perfect until next rehearsal
__End in prayer

Performance Checklist

__Establish a style of dress or look for you group
__Set up a dress rehearsal before your performance where they come dressed in performance clothing, energy and presentation

Day of Performance

__Warm up quickly and go over key parts
__Be sure to do a sound check at the venue to ensure quality sound
__Singers get dressed 1 hour before show
__Ensure singers stay way from sweets and dairy products before singing

10 Minutes Before

__Pray together as a group
__Each singer practice own vocal warm up

www.GreenwaveEntertainment.com

__Hit the stage and perform your heart out!

Recording Checklist

__If recording with a band, have session rehearsals to master all parts prior to recording

__Have your band record their parts first

__Be sure you are using a click track for timing issues

__Have a music producer to pick perfect sounds for the song

__Vocalist should be warmed up before recording

__No dairy products or cold water before or during recording

__Assure your engineer has set levels for recording

__Know the song. Don't learn the song in the studio.

__Sing!

www.GreenwaveEntertainment.com

Budget Worksheet

REVENUE	DESCRIPTION	QUANTITY	PROJECTED COST	ACTUAL COST
Music	CD Sales			
	Vinyl Sales			
	Digital Sales			
	Streaming			
	YouTube			
Live Performances	# of Shows			
Merchandise Sales	T-Shirts			
	Stickers			
	Miscellaneous			
Other	Day Job, loans, crowd-funding, etc			
	TOTAL REVENUE			
EXPENSE	**DESCRIP**		**PROJ**	**ACT**

S	TION		ECTED COST	UAL COST
Music/Merch. Costs				
	Recording/Mixing			
	CD Replication			
	Vinyl			
	Digital Distribution			
	Digital Download Card			
	Merchandise			
	TOTAL MUSIC/MERCH			
Live Shows				
	Rehearsal Space			
	Equipment			
	Posters/Flyers			
	Postage			
	Food/Gas			
	Lodging			
	Conferen			

www.GreenwaveEntertainment.com

	ce/Festival Fee			
	TOTAL LIVE SHOWS			
Publicity/Promotions				
	Graphic Design			
	Photo Shoot			
	Website			
	Publicist			
	Music Videos			
	Ads			
	TOTAL PUB/PROMO			
TOTAL EXPENSES				
TOTAL NET PROFIT	*(total revenue – total expenses = net profit)*			

www.GreenwaveEntertainment.com